NOV 1 1

D1804903

CONTENTS

Words to Know 3

1 Big and Little Beetles 4

2 Super Stingers 10

3 The Big, the Small, and the Icky 16

Many Years Ago 22

Learn More 23

Index 24

Big vs. Small

It can be scary to think of huge insects. Some can be very big, though. Others can be so tiny that they are almost invisible. All of these insect opposites are interesting no matter what size they are!

WORDS TO KNOW

burrows—Underground homes for animals; usually holes or tunnels.

larvae—The immature wingless stage of an insect during development.

parasites—An organism that lives in or off of another animal, often causing harm.

tropical—A very hot and humid climate.

1 BIG AND LITTLE BEETLES

Insects come in all sizes. The Goliath (go-LIE-ith) beetle is one big bug. It has tough armor like a tank. It sounds like a toy helicopter when it flies. It is also one of the biggest beetles in the world.

The Goliath beetle is BIG!

The feather-winged beetle is SMALL!

Some small beetles are very hard to see. Feather-winged beetles are super small. They are some of the tiniest insects in the world.

Huge Goliath beetles live in Africa. They live in the **tropical** forests.

These giant bugs can grow to more than four inches long.

Little feather-winged beetles live all over the world. They like to live under piles of dead leaves. They are so tiny that two feather-winged beetles could fit on the tip of a pencil!

Fast Fact

People often keep Goliath beetles as pets. Pet beetles eat cat or dog food.

Goliath beetles live in tropical forests.

The **larvae** (lar-VAY) of the Goliath beetle are very big. They are even larger than an adult beetle. They are also very heavy. They are some of the heaviest larvae in the world. The adult beetles are usually brown or black with white. The males have big horns. The females do not.

A female feather-winged beetle only lays one egg at a time. The egg is very large. It is half the length of an adult female. The adults have feathery wings. This is why they have that name.

Fast Fact

Most feather-winged beetles are blind.

Feather-winged beetles are so tiny that two of them can fit on the tip of a pencil!

2 SUPER STINGERS

It has many names. It is called the yak-killer hornet. It is sometimes called a sparrow bee. It is even called a tiger-head bee. The official name is the Asian giant hornet. It is the largest wasp in the world.

The giant Asian hornet is BIG!

The fairy fly is SMALL!

The smallest wasp in the world is a fairy fly. It is not as harmless as its name sounds.

The giant hornet lives in Asia. It is a large orange and black wasp. It can grow to two inches long. Its wings can be three inches across. Its stinger alone is one-quarter of an inch long!

Fairy flies are so small they are almost invisible. They live in many parts of the world. They are not only the smallest wasp, but the smallest of all insects.

Fairy flies are so small they are almost invisible. This is a photomicrograph of a fairy fly.

Asian giant hornets are strong hunters. They eat other insects. They often move in and take over honeybee hives. The adult hornets do not eat insects for food. They chew up the insects. Then they feed the chewed up prey to their larvae. The larvae then ooze a liquid. This is what the giant hornets eat!

Tiny fairy flies are not a danger to humans. They are only a danger to other insects. These small wasps are **parasites**. They lay their own eggs inside other insects' eggs. This destroys those insects' eggs.

Fast Fact

Hornet juice is a favorite sports drink in Asia. It is supposed to be much like the ooze that the hornets eat. Some Asian athletes believe the drink gives them energy and strength.

The giant Asian hornet can be two inches long!

3 THE BIG, THE SMALL AND THE ICKY

Few people like cockroaches. They are seen as pests. However, some people keep one kind of roach as a pet. It is the giant burrowing cockroach. It is one of the biggest roaches in the world.

The giant burrowing cockroach is BIG!

The ant cockroach, seen here on the back of an ant, is SMALL!

Another cockroach can barely be seen. It is the ant cockroach. It is also one of the smallest insects anywhere in the world.

Giant burrowing cockroaches live in Australia. They can fit in the palm of a human hand. They grow to more than three inches long. They are not like many roaches. They are clean and have no odor. They are slow-moving insects.

Ant cockroaches live with leafcutter ants. They live in North America. The ants do not seem to mind sharing their home with these tiny roaches. These tiny roaches only grow to a tenth of an inch long.

Ant cockroaches live with leafcutter ants. Leafcutter ants take the leaves back to their nest.

Some cockroaches have wings. The giant burrowing cockroach does not. Like its name suggests, it lives in **burrows**. These huge roaches burrow in sandy soil. They eat dead plant and animal matter.

Ants act like taxis for the ant cockroach. The small cockroaches jump on the backs of soldier ants. They lick the backs of the ants for food. This does not hurt the ants. In fact, they do not seem to notice at all. They simply walk around with the cockroaches on their backs.

Fast Fact

The ant cockroach is nearly blind. It uses its sense of smell to find its way around.

Some people keep giant burrowing cockroaches as pets!

MANY YEARS AGO...

Just the thought of a giant insect gives most people the creeps. *Meganeura* (me-gah-NYUR-ah) would have sent them screaming. It was a giant dragonfly! It lived millions of years ago. It was the largest flying insect that ever lived. *Meganeura* looked like modern dragonflies. But it was bigger than most birds today. Its wingspan would have been more than two feet across.

This giant dragonfly lived millions of years ago!

LEARN MORE

Books

Hall, Margaret. *Wasps*. Mankato, Minn.: Capstone Press, 2006.

Packard, Mary. *Goliath Beetle: One of the World's Heaviest Insects*. New York: Bearport Publishing, 2007.

Twist, Clint. *Cockroaches*. Milwaukee, Wisc.: Gareth Stevens Publishing, 2005.

Internet Addresses

Amazing Pests

<http://dev.pestworldforkids.org/guide.html>

Amazing Roach Facts

<http://yucky.discovery.com/flash/roaches/pg000097.html>

INDEX

Africa, 5
ant cockroach, 17, 18, 19, 20
Asia, 11, 14
Asian giant hornet, 10, 11, 14, 15
Australia, 17

fairy fly, 11, 12, 13, 14
feather-winged beetle, 5, 6, 8, 9

giant burrowing cockroach, 16, 17, 20, 21
goliath beetle, 4, 5, 6, 7, 8

leafcutter ants, 18, 19

Meganeura, 22

North America, 18

Bailey Books
an imprint of
Enslow Publishers, Inc.
40 Industrial Road
Box 398
Berkeley Heights, NJ 07922
USA

http://www.enslow.com

In Memory of Khrystian.
These books are dedicated to the students of Greentree.

Bailey Books, an imprint of Enslow Publishers, Inc.

Copyright © 2011 by Enslow Publishers, Inc.

All rights reserved.

No part of this book may be reproduced by any means without the written permission of the publisher.

Library of Congress Cataloging-in-Publication Data

Mitchell, Susan K.
  Biggest vs. smallest incredible insects / Susan K. Mitchell.
       p. cm. — (Biggest vs. smallest animals)
  Includes bibliographical references and index.
  Summary: "Provides information on the biggest and smallest beetles, wasps, and cockroaches". Provided by publisher.
  ISBN 978-0-7660-3583-6
  1. Insects—Juvenile literature. 2. Body size—Juvenile literature. I. Title. II. Title: Biggest ver smallest incredible insects.
  QL467.2.M584 2010
  595.7—dc22
                                                        2009001677

Printed in the United States of America

062010 Lake Book Manufacturing, Inc., Melrose Park, IL

10 9 8 7 6 5 4 3 2 1

To Our Readers: We have done our best to make sure all Internet Addresses in this book were active and appropriate when we went to press. However, the author and the publisher have no control over and assume no liability for the material available on those Internet sites or on othe Web sites they may link to. Any comments or suggestions can be sent by e-mail to comments@ enslow.com or to the address on the back cover.

Every effort has been made to locate all copyright holders of material used in this book. If any errors omissions have occurred, corrections will be made in future editions of this book.

♻ Enslow Publishers, Inc., is committed to printing our books on recycled paper. The paper in eve book contains 10% to 30% post-consumer waste (PCW). The cover board on the outside of each contains 100% PCW. Our goal is to do our part to help young people and the environment too!

Illustration Credits: © 1999 Artville, LLC, pp. 6, 12, 18; Scott Camazine/Photo Researchers, pp. 10, 15; Bruce Davidson/naturepl.com, pp. 1 (big), 4; Enslow Publishers, Inc., illustrations of monkeys and children throughout the book; Reyes Garcia III, USDA Agricultural Research Ser Bugwood.org, p. 11; © Lightwave Photography, Inc./Animals Animals-Earth Scenes, p. 19; Mich McCoy/Photo Researchers, Inc., p. 16; Piotr Naskrecki/Minden Pictures, p. 7, backcover; © OSF Atkinson, Kathy/Animals Animals-Earth Scenes, p. 21; Dr. Harold Rose/Photo Researchers, Inc. p. 13; M. Seymour, Louisiana State University, pp. 9, 17; © Surface Vision, p. 22; © Brian Valen pp. 1 (small), 5.

Cover Illustration: Bruce Davidson/naturepl.com (Goliath beetle) and © Brian Valentine (feather-winged beetle).